# The STEM Sisters

## Celebrating Women Voices in STEM

*By Samaira Jain*

**Author's Note**

The book *The STEM Sisters* is dedicated to women in STEM, Science and Math. It tells about the stories of mathematicians, their awards, challenges, and life. I have greatly enjoyed and soaked the true essence of mathematics as a subject. It has not only enhanced my problem-solving skills but also extended my appreciation for logic and abstract thinking. Mathematics has taught me to approach challenges strategically. Through *The STEM Sisters*, I aim to amplify these hidden voices and poems, hoping to shed light on the incredible Mathematicians around the world. I was encouraged by my achievement in SIMOC (Singapore International Math Olympiad Challenge) where I bagged the silver medal in both the challenges. At an international level, it was intriguing to see how students around the world were connected by the global language of Math. Irrespective of what everyone spoke, it was heartwarming to see how they all understood symbols, numbers and equations. We were all connected by the mutual understanding of logic and numeracy that Math brought to our lives.

However, *The STEM Sisters* did not occur overnight. Truly, Rome is not built in a day! To

begin with, I am deeply grateful to my parents: Mrs. Somya Jain and Mr. Ajay Jain as they filled me with enthusiasm to write this book. They recognized my mathematical-literary talent, and helped me get the best possible guidance to give this book a home.
I'm also grateful to my mentor, Ms. Shalini Gulyani, who helped me throughout the writing and editing process. In addition to giving me ideas, ma'am also helped me compile my work and uplift a voice I never knew that I had. I'm also deeply indebted to my best friend, Arika, for being my rock and source of joy throughout this process. Your laughter and positive affirmation fuelled my thinking process, and I don't think the book would've been possible without you.

I want to thank everybody from the bottom of my heart who has been a contribution to this ebook. Also, thank you dear reader(s) for reading this book and enjoying the poems. I hope we can come together to appreciate our STEM sisters!

In Gratitude,
Samaira Jain
January 2025

# Malala: The Ship of Courage

When I held her in my arms,
A rosebud so glorious and mild—
Glistening under the golden sunshine
My first child
My hopes, my aspirations and my joy
My dreams came true that day
A mother was born and brought to life
I am a human being
Of two different worlds
Once a wife, and now a mother—
Maybe I am not educated well
But I as a mother I take a pledge that
"My daughter Malala Yousafzai
Will have a good education
A good life
She will rise above the pots and pans,
And not be confined to the kitchen like me"
Soon into her teenagehood,
My daughter got death threats
I felt scared, frightened, frustrated and uncertain
For her life,
I knew that the Taliban was capable of doing
anything!
This was not just a death threat but a—
Major war between the Taliban and Malala
I could not stop Malala because she was fighting
Fighting for a reason and a good cause

The cause that Malala was fighting for
Was not so easy to fight for
She stood up for girls education
Making each girl successful
The Taliban would destroy the temples of education
With their bad bombs,
And most of the all, they would not let girls study
My worst fears came true!
On her way back home from school
As my little girl sang with her friends—
A masked gunman boarded the bus with a gun
The Taliban gunman asked 'Who is Malala?'
The Taliban gunman, shot her point blank
One bullet entered and exited her head
Her clothes all drenched in red
My daughter was left nearly lifeless
The light in my eyes went dull
My daughter is a fighter and so will I fight for her
From one hospital to another
Many surgeries happened
After ten torturous days
She opened her eyes at Birmingham
I have heard that ships in the harbour,
Must leave the harbour,
Because that's not where ships are supposed to be,
My daughter! My dear! She left her harbour,
And ended up in the hospital bed!
I should be proud! But instead,
My eyes are lowered in shame and regret.

As a mother, should I have stopped her?
Should I have held her hand?
When she wielded the microphone to give her
speech,
Should I have sealed her lips?
As I stand outside the surgery room—
And remove my headscarf, I hold it to the skies—
As if it is my offering to God,
I hear my heart speak to me,
"My dear daughter had sailed
Through the turbulent waters
My daring daughter continues to sail
Through the storms of seas
My dynamic daughter will never turn back
She will continue to explore new horizons,
She is a ship who must leave the harbour—
Of comfort! And fight for the rights of girls!
Cause that is what courageous and confident ships,
Like Malala are meant for!

# The Queen of Indian Mathematics

A calculator was born
Not it but she
Not a normal it is a special one
Called as a human calculator
This calculator had an
Immense passion for numbers
She, she was born on 4th of November in 1929
Her name was Shakuntala Devi
The first woman mathematician in India
And even known as
The queen of Indian Mathematics
From the Guinness Book of World Record to the
'Most Distinguished Woman of the Year' from the
University of Philippine
And then to the
Ramanujan Mathematical Genius Award
In Washington D.C in 1988
She was able to calculate lengthy calculations
In her head swiftly
And without any calculator
In a split second
Shakuntala would complete massive calculations
Her noteworthy calculations included
Cube roots, seventh roots
And the great and rapid multiplication
Of two thirteen digit numbers
She a humble personality

Shakuntala Devi an inspiration for all
Shakuntala cherished to simplify the magic of
arithmetic
She playing in a role of three people
A mother, a wife and a genius mathematician

# The Princess of Parallelograms

Augusta Ada Byron
An another name of Ada Lovelace
Ada was an enthusiast for maths and computers
She was the one who created the first computer
code
What all she has gone from
Like when as a kid at her birth
The marriage of her mother and father was over
The first computer programmer
She was an associate of Charles Babbage
Not only success she had in her journey of life
But this journey of life had many difficult problems
Problems made this journey an adventure
Adding more and more twists to it
Looks interesting in hearing
But has much more to it and she has faced it
She also invented the first algorithm for a machine
She invented this in the 1800s
Ada didn't win any awards in her lifetime
And her contributions were largely ignored
Till the 1950s

At that time Ada's role in the
Birth of computer programming was finally
recognized
In the year of 1843 Lovelace translated

A French paper that an Italian mathematician
Luigi Menabrea wrote about the Analytical Engine
Ada added a thousand of words
Of her own notes to the paper
She realised that the Analytical Engine
Would carry out an
Extensive sequence of mathematical operations
Ada Lovelace Day is celebrated annually
On the second Tuesday of October
This day is celebrated annually
To celebrate and raise awareness of the
contributions
Of women to STEM fields
She was not only a contributor to Mathematics
But also the Founder of Scientific Computing
Born on 10 December 1815
And died at the age of 36
Ada Lovelace is buried inside the
Church of St. Mary Magdalene in the
Small English town of Hucknall
Her coffin was placed side by side
With that of her father,
Who also passed away at the age of 36
As said in the honour of Ada Lovelace Day
That the brain of yours is something more than
merely mortal
As the time will show

# **<u>Mrs. Universe Computer</u>**

A person or a woman
Same thing but different
By their genders
A Person can be both
Male and Female
A woman is only a Female
Well, the human being
I'm talking about was a
A woman born on
August 26, 1918
An American mathematician
Her name was Katherine Johnson
She started from Maths
But then geometry in Math
Opened her intelligence wider
Making her an enthusiast of
Both Science and Math
She calculated and analyzed
The flight paths of many spacecrafts
She worked in NASA
She helped NASA
Send astronauts to the moon
And return them back to the Earth
Which is their home sweet home
Katherine overcame
Racial and gender hurdles
That helped make giant hops

For humankind
There is one unique thing about her
She was in when she was 15 only
Think about it!
She graduated with honors
At the age of 18
She taught Black students Math
And broke down barriers
In a world where doors were shut
But she knocked and knocked
And then she opened them
For others to follow
Her work was invisible to most
But without her, the stars might not have aligned
For history to shine so bright
She didn't seek fame,
She sought truth in numbers
Guiding rockets, reaching for the sky
Her legacy is not just in the equations
But in the courage to defy
She proved that a woman, a Black woman,
Could write her own future
And chart a path
For generations to come
Her name, Katherine Johnson
Will echo through time forever.

# The Mathematician, Master and Changer

A great Indian mathematician
Present with us till now
To support us and guide us
She is the one
Who's name is
Sujatha Ramdorai
She was born in 1962
Her day and month of birth
Being invisible and unknown to us
She is a professor of mathematics
Who taught in the
Tata Institute of Fundamental Research previously
And now she is!
Professor of mathematics and Canada Research
Chair
At the University of British Columbia at Canada
Sujatha Ramdorai is an algebraic number theorist
She is known for her work on
Iwasawa theory
Sujatha Ramodorai discovered
Her love for mathematics
When she was in the primary years
She studied at the
Tata Institute of Fundamental Research,
St. Joseph's College and
Annamalai University

Sujatha Ramdorai is the first and only Indian
Who won the
ICTP Ramanujan Award in 2006
She also won the
**Shanti Swaroop Bhatnagar Award in 2004**
And not the least but
The Padma Shri award in 2023
She has faced and continues to face challenges but
She never stopped over there
She turned them to invisible dust
That wouldn't stop her way to her goal
She found new challenges
But she turned them to
A sparkle of joy to her life
To make her realize
That she is capable of doing everything
No matter any bull comes in the way
No matter any snow that falls in the way
No matter what
She understood the
Challenges that women faced
Making them understand that
You are capable of doing it
And go according to yourself
Do not listen to what people say
Sujatha Ramdorai is an inspiration
For all women till now
And she will continue being one
For all the women of the future generations

Not only women but even girls of
The past, the present and the future
Her story has been full of might
Is full of might
And will remain full of might
Her name shines bright
Whether it is under the sun
Or the moon
She is a guide for her followers
The girls or the women
But she will guide both
Making both successful
And full of pride
Sujatha Ramdorai will continue to inspire
And to become a mathematician
Will become a desire for them
She is a symbol of
Courage, grace
And most of all knowledge
The generations which are yet to come
Her impact will be known
To all people especially women and girls
She's a name and sign of
Resilience, wisdom and care
Sujatha Ramdorai gives an opportunity
To those who want and dare to fly
And never stop no matter how high they fly

# <u>A Star Beyond The Universe</u>

The earliest mathematician
Not male but female
The one I am talking about
Is a person
Who lived in Alexandria
Located in Egypt
She is astronomer, philosopher and
Of course a mathematician
The person I am talking about
Must be known to one and all
Her name was Hypatia
She was born
In the 355 CE
And died in the March 415 AD
She has had many successes
She refined the many scientific instruments,
Wrote math textbooks
And not the least but even
Developed an even more well regulated way
Of long division
Hypatia was lucky
Because she was born to
A famous mathematician and philosopher
She had more freedom
Than many girls
That also because of her respected father

Her father was Theon of Alexandria
Most women from her area
And other places also
Were not even allowed to study math and science
And they were denied to engage in politics
Hypatia became one of the first women
Who studied and taught
Maths, astronomy and
Not the least but philosophy also
Hypatia grew up
With only her father
Theon of Alexandria
He had a dream to
Raise the perfect human
Her father
Taught Hypatia everything
From geometry to algebra
To astronomy
And even how to become
An influential speaker
Which would inspire people
To follow her and
So did happen
People followed Hypatia
Not normal people like me
But great mathematicians
And great astronomers
Were influenced for centuries
They were influenced

They are fired with enthusiasm
They will never stop to spur
Hypatia gave an public voice
To women for the first time
To stand up for themselves
To prove that they are smart and
Have intelligent thoughts like men
Or even better than them
To show that they are capable
Of doing everything in this world
They are a multi tasker
Her notes on math and astronomy
Helped modern mathematicians and astronomers
To come up with even more advanced theories
That are still used till the date of today
And will be used in the future
They will be advanced further
For the future generations
To make this world a better place
To live for every single person
Alive on this planet
Her brilliance shines beyond stars
Beyond the sun
And what-not
In every equation she has solved and created
Her spirit appears
Hypatia is a shining ideal
To inspire one and all
For every single woman

For every single mind
On this planet
Whether in the past
Whether in the present
Whether in the future
To embolden each and everyone
To dream, to aspire, and to discover

# The Name Shining Through The Black Hole

Both,
A natural philosopher
And a french mathematician
The first female scientist
To be published in the
Paris Academy
Her name was Émilie du Châtelet
Born on 17 December in 1706
And died at the age of 42
She died because of
Complications that happened
Only 6 days after giving birth
Her greatest achievement was
The translation and commentary on
Isaac Newton's Principia Mathematica
She also discovered that
Kinetic energy is equal to one half times
The mass times the velocity squared
Émilie du Châtelet was also
The first female scientist
To be published in the
Paris Academy
She got influenced by three people
But she grew bigger and smarter than them
Because that was only an inspiration for her
She wanted to create herself as an inspiration
Maybe the past had gone

But for the present
Anf for the future
To make women privileged for everything
On this world
To give them the opportunity to do
Every single thing
She wanted them
To explore
To do
To make themselves and
The future generation
Open to everything
To stand up for women
To speak for women
To give other women the base to
Stand up for themselves and raise their voices
Émilie du Châtelet gave them the right
To fight
Fight for everything they want
Fight for themselves
To get what they deserve
To be allowed to
Widen their mind
Gain more knowledge
Learn more
Whether in cooking
Whether in clothing
Whether in math
Whether in science

Whether in all of them
Émilie du Châtelet
Made other people understand that
She saw those challenges
Overcome them
Was stuck under them
Because she couldn't cross them
Neither from crawling nor from jumping
Day by day,
People were inspired from her
And kept on going just like her
They saw her success
And her challenges
But they didn't think
That they will face this
And give up after that
They thought that they
Will try to face challenges
But there is no life without challenges
They thought again
And made their decision
That if they are stuck in this challenge
They will continue
Whether they fall a million times
Whether they are struck by lighting
Whether they are getting burnt in fire
They will continue to run
Her name is a symbol
Of equations, failures,

And most all success
Her brilliance inspires
Many,
And one of them being me
She reminds that knowledge
Can be given to anyone
Whether male or female
Whether animals, who have no gender
She is a reminder that one single mind
Can change the whole world
Her name, Émilie du Châtelet
Will never be forgotten
Not in the 1800
Not in the 1900
Not in the 2000
Not in the 2010
Not in the 2020
Not in the 2030
Not in this whole journey
Till the earth exists
Émilie du Châtelet,
She was a achiever
A risk taker whose name
Shines through the black hole

# **The Quiet Revolution**

A woman who faced
Lack of support from her family
This woman was unable
To make a career out of Mathematics
But she was independent
This woman's name was
Sophie Germain
She was born on
April 1st 1776
She was a french mathematician
A physicist
And when a kid
She was an avid reader
Her parents were
Ambroise-Francois and Marie Germain
Her family was wealthy
But the amount of
Opportunities for her were zero
She got had lack of support
From both
Her family and society
Sophie Germain initially
Pretended to be a male
To overcome social isolation
Her academic advisor was
The prince of mathematics
Carl Friedrich Gauss

She won many prestigious awards
Importantly,
She won the Paris Academy of Sciences
In 1816
She contributed
To the study of 3 specific things
Those being
Acoustics, elasticity and
The theory of numbers
Sophie Germain,
Used to wrap herself in the blankets
Light the candles
And study
Soon her parents realized
Her immense passion for numbers
And let her live
Let take part in various competitions
To be in the spotlight
To be known to all
She was inspired
Now she is the one who inspires
In the time to come
The name 'Sophie Germain'
Will echo beyond the earth
Beyond the Milky Way Galaxy
Beyond the universe
Beyond the horizons
Her story told in whispered winds
A tale of triumph that never ends.

# <u>The Risk Taker</u>

The first Woman President
Of the USA?
No, the first Woman President
Of the American Mathematical Society
Not a regular but an American Mathematician
Who entered San Diego College
And then transferred to the
University of California at Berkeley
She was Julia Robinson
Born on 8 December 1919
She was the second daughter amongst the three
To Helen Hall Bowman and Ralph Bowers
Bowman
She had two sisters
The elder one being Constance
And the younger one being Billie
She succeeded many times
But also lost sometimes
Sometime she faced challenges
But she rose above them
Becoming a risk taker
She was the
First female mathematician to be elected
To the National Academy of Sciences
Julia Robinson contributed to the
Solution of Hilbert's Tenth Problem
Julia Robinson was a part of the tem of the

American Academy of Arts and Sciences
She also made a worth of attention contribution to
Solving the travelling salesman problem
She faced one major challenge out of those many which
Affected her education but she
Never gave up
Julia Robinson endured agony
At the age of nine she was stricken first
Through Scarlet fever and then rheumatic fever
And after several relapses
It only forced her to
Spend a year in the bed
As a result she lost almost 2 years of school
And there were more
Incoming serious and lifelong consequences
For her health
Which at the end of the day
Even affected her life
When Julia robinson reached her final years of schooling
She was left as the only girl in her mathematics and physics class
Juila Robinson was not just a mathematician
She was a explorer
She is known because
Of the equation she solved
The barriers she broke into pieces
And the gates she opened for

The future stages of life
Her life will not stop inspiring people
Her work will continue to show people the way
Julia Robinson's place in the old days
Will never be forgotten by anyone
The titles she got throughout her space
Were not names
But her achievements, success and inspiration
For not only other people but her too
They were the highest point of her lifetime
With courage, brilliance, inspiration
And most of all success
They were achievements
To inform her she is not less
But even more unique than all
And tell her to chase more after knowledge
Her story in only one amongst many
But this one also known with a lot of fame
Showing the world
That no matter how many struggles
Julia Robinson faces
She never gave up and cried on her knees
She taught people and continues to teach people
That the heart of a true mathematician
Never abandons something they follow
Through their heart and mind
It beats with the rhythm of discovery
Like it is a treasure for them
And boundless search for truth.

# <u>Whispers of Numbers</u>

A British Mathematician
Who lived for 97 years
Can you believe it?
A mathematician
Who was honoured
Honoured by Queen Elizabeth II
She was a marvelous woman in Math
Her name was Mary Cartwright
Born on 17 December in 1900
She lived for 97 years
With tons of achievements
She won a lot of awards
She won the De Morgan Medal in 1968
Mary Cartwright was the first woman
To win the Sylvester Medal in 1964
To serve on the Council of the Royal Society
To be the President of the Mathematical Association
And not the least but also
To be the President of the London Mathematical
Society
She took the lead research in
Chaos theory and most if all
The butterfly effect
She lived for 97 years
I have faced so many challenges being 11 only
Think about her

Mary Cartwright must have
Faced so many challenges
But she rose above them
Forgot about them
Once she left the ship from the harbour
She stopped at harbours when she was injured
Or faced challenges
But the day the problem was solved
She left the harbour again
All set for her next ups and downs
And if at all
She could not
Put that failure into the air to disappear
Mary Cartwright would
Leave it behind that harbour and
Continue her journey
Which was made
To explore
Explore,
New horizons
New awards
New challenges
New failures
And,
New downs that would drown her
Into the great deep seas
But she wouldn't give up
For her the journey was endless
The voyage was never completed

Each wave was a lesson
Each storm was a endeavour
Through every wave and storm
She continued to sail with
Grace, courage, patience and possibilities
Each try was a success sometimes
Sometime a failure
But she turned it into
Hope, joy, ambition and
A stepping stone to success
Whether it was a success
Whether a failure
She turned into a space
To dream
To strive
To keep the spark of math alive
And keep sparkle in her life
Without mathematics there was no shine
But she brought that shine to many lives
Keeping them on the earth
Her ship has sailed beyond our vision
But,
Her light still burns bright
Beyond the quasar
She is a legend of numbers and chart
And courage, resilience, and a thousand hearts

# The First Female Maths Professor

The First Female Maths Professor
Not of only a country
But the whole world
A russian mathematician
Her name was Sofya Kovalevskaya
Born on 15 January in 1850
And died at the age of 41
Her lifetime was short
But she never knew it was so short
Her lifetime being short
Did not affect her achievements
Even after a short lifetime
She achieved
Achieved many things
She won many awards
She was the first woman in
Modern Europe to get a doctorate in mathematics
She was the first to join and become a part of
The editorial board of a scientific journal
The last but no the least
Sofya Kovalevskaya was the first to be
An appointed professor of mathematics
She succeeded
She lost
She tried to overcome
She overcame sometime
She could not overcome sometimes

She focused on succeeds
And sometimes failures
But she did not stop after that failure
She removed her focus from that failure
And continued on to turn
Those failures into success
It became -1 after failure
But,
She made it +2 after success
She brought it up 2 points and
Made it success
She focused on the outcome
After the success
Not the failure
She converted into the positive result
That got her 2 more points
More closer to victory
She left behind her failures
She died because of Pneumonia
It was a hard time
But the achievements she made
Before that
Were tremendous
As she has so much success
Before death
And if she stayed longer
Maybe she would be known even more
With many awards
Inspiring more people

Her path was full of curves
She hugged the struggles
And felt it at something positive
Not negative
It was something she loved
Her name was not only
Known for numbers
But for the barriers she broke
The success she had
She was thriving and
Breaking barriers
Which created those
Ups and downs
In her life
And those made her life too
She passed at 41
But her impact
That changed the world
In some way
Still remains in the world
Her achievements were not only
The medals and certificates she got
Sofya Kovalevskaya proved
That brilliance in any work
Has no limits
Whether it is hers too
She proved that it has no boundaries
And no time
Her life was brief

Her little change still burns
And shines bright
Sofya Kovalevskaya's name
Endures forever as a symbol as a sign
And as a tigers scratch on a rock
To mark the way the went through
She is a symbol
Of  bravery, resistance and success

# **<u>Echoes of Symmetry</u>**

The Mother of Mathematics
A brilliant mathematician
She was the
Daughter of a German Mathematician
Her name was Emmy Noether
Born on 23 March 1882
Her parents were Max Noether
A german mathematician
Her mother was Amalia Kaufmann
Emmy Noether is recognized
As one of the
Greatest mathematician of
The 20th century
She won
She lost
Both many times
She faced challenges
She overcame them
She was stuck because of them
Because she couldn't jump over it
Because she couldn't cross it from the underground
Emmy Noether received
The Ackermann–Teubner Memorial Award
She made innovatory contributions
To abstract algebra
And also
Theoretical physics

These topics she learnt
Were not easy
To learn
She faced many challenges
Despite them she continued her journey
To become a mathematician
Known to one and all on this world
Maybe,
Maybe during her lifetime
Her work was overshadowed
But now she is recognized
As a great mathematician
She was known in the past but overshadowed
She is known in the present
With full fame
There will be new mathematicians who join people
Like Julia Robinson
Like Katherine Johnson
Like Shakuntla Devi
Like Sujatha Ramdorai
Like Ada Lovelace
Like Mary Cartwright
Like Hypatia
Like so many other
But her name will continue
Shining bright
In the solar eclipse
And even brighter in the lunar eclipse
Her work on the

Noether's Theorem
Connects the fundamental laws
Of physics
To the concept
Symmetry
This impacted the fields
Of quantum mechanics
And general relativity
She is called the creative mathematical genius
This name was given by the great brain
Albert Einstein was the one
Who gave Emmy Noether this name
She survived till 53 in this world
Imagine 53 ups and downs
Means many failures
But she was the one who never gave up
She made change in the whole world
Till now there mark that she was alive
That she impacted the world
In some way or the other
That she lived for 53 years but
Her impact lasting till today
She was a trailblazer!
She is known as a trailblazer!
She will be known as a trailblazer
In the future
To one all
Woman or girl or man or boy
She is legacy

Of resilience, passion,
Encouragement, determination and ambition

# <u>Raman Parimala: Indian By Nationality But International At Heart</u>

An Indian Mathematician
Who is a
Supreme and powerful algebraist
Her name is
Raman Parimala
She was born on
21st November 1948
She was a professor at the
TATA Institute of Fundamental Research
Her research uses various tools
From number theory
To algebraic theory
And even topology
She studied hard
To become an achiever
To win a lot of awards
She had her education 3 different places
All being very famous and unique
From the Noether's Lecture Award
To the Shanti Swarup Bhatnagar Prize in 1987
To an honorary doctorate from the
University of Lausanne in 1999,
To the Srinivasa Ramanujan Birth Centenary Award
in 2003
Raman Parimala has held visiting positions

At the Swiss Federal Institute of Technology (ETH)
in Zürich,
The University of Lausanne,
University of California-Berkeley,
University of Chicago, Ohio State,
And even,
The University of Paris at Orsay
Two more to go,
In 2005 she was appointed
The Asa Griggs Candler Professor of Mathematics
At Emory University in Atlanta, Georgia
And currently
A distinguished Professor
At the Emory University
And coming to the most notable achievement she
had
Was publishing the first example of a
Nontrivial quadratic space over an affine plane
Such prestigious awards she got
Only being 76 years old
Think when she gets older and older
She is able to to do this
Because she didn't care what other people said
She wanted to achieve her goal
She is known as an Indian mathematician
But by heart a International mathematician
Who has received various international awards,
Her talent is not limited to
The tricolor soil of our country

It is instead
Wide-spanning and global

# When Mathematics and Myths Mingle Together

*The Tale of Nadim, The Mathematician*

Singapore,
It was a small fishing village nestled by the sea
People lived simple lives
A normal living
Nothing was complicated
Day by day as time passed
Their peace was disrupted by a giant evil swordfish
With evil and wide open eyes
The wicked swordfish would attack and kill
everybody
Who dared to ventured too close to the water
As this time passed the supply of fishes
Dwindled and dwindled
Village leaders along with the Raja decided
To take over and kill the cruel enormous swordfish
They prepared and trained but on the day
They went to kill the swordfish
The swordfish was fully ready for the war to start
It started killing the soldiers one by one
And almost none of them were left
There was complete silence
But then appeared a little boy named Nadim
Nadim was clever minded
And had a great passion for numbers

He went to the soldier and told him the idea
The soldier went to the king
And asked for the approval
The king approved and they prepared the catapult
They took it to the shore and waited for the
swordfish
To come to exact coordinates of the shore
Which were ( 5, 4 )
They waited long and then it finally came
To the exact coordinate after 2 hours
They launched the catapult
The swordfish was demolished and killed
Nadim was taken to the royal palace
The king awarded him by a trophy and blessings
He gave him the trophy of the
**_'Best Coordinate Master Mathematician'_**
Nadim thanked the king
He became a contributor to the royal palace
Nadim was awarded many trophies by the royal
palace

*A Miscellaneous Mist*


*Samaira's Previous Writings*

# <u>Poem Response: To 'Crumble' by Lisa Westberg Peters</u>

Why should I not crumble?

Said the sandstone

I am at sixes and sevens.

Truly woebegone!

Can you ask the wind to stop blowing?

Can you ask the river to stop flowing?

Can you ask the rain to stop pattering?

Can you ask the milk to stop spattering?

Can you ask yourself to stop instructing me?

And behaving as if you are busier than a bee

If you do this,

I will try my best.

To change from a man of straw

To a man of steel

This truly is my heartfelt appeal.

To stop bossing me around

I repeat again, stop bossing me around!

Said the sandstone, with a final sigh!

Let me live, or else I'll cry.

I contain light within me like a firefly.

After all, everything that crumbles

Is not weak!

There is great strength in being weak.

## The True Power of Friendship

*Dedicated to Arika Bhatia*

She and me
Is the example
I would take for friendship
Far out or close together
We stay with each other

We have magnetic power
That always has kept us together
One at the north and one at the south
But always we keep
Our hands together

We started together
Still keep together
But will never end together
Because the friendship
Will always remain joined forever

We are best friends
We are the people you would want to meet
We are the world to each other
And that's why
We are "WE"

# **Rings of Time**

*Published in Elysian Magazine, Shiv Nadar School, Faridabad*

"Zzzz" went the hoop sliding away from me. It crashed into the wall in front of me and made me wince. I was trying to learn the technique of palm hooping, but the hoop went flying in the air. If I had not been careful enough, it would have banged into the mirror in front of me, making the glass crash into a million smithereens. I was scared while learning because the hoop had already hit me multiple times!

It had been almost two weeks since I was learning the first technique, and I still did not get it. I was at sixes and sevens and wondered whether there was an issue with my grasping power. I felt bad and nervous because everyone in my class had almost gotten the first two techniques. My teacher came to me and told me to buy a hoop for my home so I could practice at home. She also told me to become confident and not get scared.

"Tringgg tringgg," the bell rang as it was time for breakfast. My friends and I wore our shoes and moved to our class to get our tiffin boxes and then moved to the dining hall. All of us were garrulous and had camaraderie among us. Mysha was a gourmand, and she ate her food before we even started. I asked them how they got all the techniques so fast. All of them had different responses.

"I do hula-hoop classes with our teacher," said Mysha.
"I have a hoop at my home; I practice with it," replied Kaira.
"I feel a surge of confidence within me and do not feel nervous, so I can achieve my goal," answered Meher.

All of them also told me that they set a goal every day for achieving one technique.

Thereafter, the day went on, and we continued studying. When the bell rang, heralding the end of the day, I sat in the car, and on my way home, I thought about what my friends told me during breakfast. Finally, I reached home and went inside.

My mother asked me, "What are you thinking about, Samaira?"
I replied, "I am just thinking about hula hoops."

That evening, when my father came from his office, I asked him to buy me a hoop. He agreed and told me that he's making me join a hoop class. It was telepathic congruity! I was ebullient and started jumping on the bed. However, it wasn't entirely a bed of roses for me! My father added that he would see the outcome and analyze my progress after every week, and if my progress wasn't satisfactory, he was going to make me leave the class.

I decided to agree and obey my father. I also took my friends' advice to get better. From that day onwards, I started practicing hooping for around 1 hour every day. During weekends, when I did not have school, I burned the midnight oil.

I saw the change in myself and thanked my friends and my parents for giving me such a great idea. Their blandishments helped me a lot. Since then, hula-hoop has become my foremost passion. I got to know the importance of confidence, hard work, and many more things with the help of my friends, my parents, and my great mentors.

I was thankful to have them because they were the ones who helped me overcome my problems, and because of them, I was promoted from the beginner batch to the advanced batch. Now, when I compare myself in hula-hoop right now to how I was earlier, I see a big change. I feel more confident—but not overconfident—because I learned that overconfidence can also have a detrimental effect.

My mentor told me that she has also struggled a lot in her life, not only in hooping but also in other things. She told me that my struggles in hula hooping are only the tip of the iceberg. Therefore, my hula-hoop journey was truly memorable, as because of it, I acquired different life lessons from different people.

It was truly a ring of time—where the anxieties of the past, learnings of the present, and aspirations of the future were gracefully connected.

# Exploring the Familial Garden of Time

*Published in Elysian Magazine, Shiv Nadar School, Faridabad*

*"Goo goo ga ga"* said the two-year-old twin sisters as they clapped their hands to applaud their elder brother for the interesting and amusing show. The brother's name was Ayaan and he was very happy to know that his sisters enjoyed the show. Ayaan planned to give an amazing and appealing show everyday to keep his sisters, Ayra and Arya entertained. All of them were alone the whole day because their parents were working and didn't have time to play with them.

It was Ayaan's summer vacation so he took the duty of handling Arya and Ayra. Ayaan had always wanted twin sisters so he always took care and did not want a babysitter to babysit them and rule on them. Ayaan was a responsible, caring, helpful and open-minded boy. He never took down and said a no to things that his parents suggested. This was only because their family was educated well and had manners unlike some of the children in Ayaan's school.

Their ancestors always expected to make a clean break. It was like a rule that everybody in their family was given some lessons. These lessons were about how to be a well behaved human being. It talked about caring and respecting each other. There were some quotes explained, real life examples and most of all life lessons like 'Nothing is free in the world' and many more. The lessons were the life lessons and learning for the whole family that were carried on from the past to the future and would be carried out further to future generations of their family. The life lessons were from their ancestors who lived during World War 1 and then World War 2 and then continued being passed on. Every family member had these lessons from his/her parents and Ayaan had the same lesson. All of the people from their family, the ancestors, the current generations and the future generations had a family tree with deep roots. The family was really bonded well.

Ayaan planned to start telling his younger sisters about that from the start so it's easy and not time taking for his parents. It was very easy forAyaan's, Arya's and Ayra's parents to handle them. The parents even gave the twin sisters a lesson before time. Both of the sisters got the rules and became diligent and hard working just like their brother. Their parents thought that they were eligible and civilised to go on an international trip. Both of them also thought that the apple doesn't fall far from the tree. They thought of taking a small break from work and going on a trip abroad. Anyways, they were irritated and exhausted because of the major heat in Delhi.

They booked the tickets for Zurich in Switzerland. Their flight was in the next two days. They packed their clothings and other needs. After two days, they were off to Switzerland. The 8 hours and 30 minutes flight was filled with different kinds of feelings. In the first 2 hours they were confused and bored because they could not decide what to play. When they reached Zurich, it felt cool, refreshing and relaxing. They took a taxi and went to the hotel. Ayaan went to his mom and told his mom that the lessons that were given to him were very useful and helpful for him. Ayaan thanked his mother and promised to follow the life lessons given by his parents and give the same life lessons to other people so that they also became kind, caring, helpful and develop other positive behaviours. "Like father, like son," replied Ayaan's mother. Their mother was also very happy to hear that and hugged them tightly. 'You are a chip of the old block because you resemble your mother' said Ayaan, Ayra and Ayra's father to the two twin sisters, Ayra and Arya.

Ayaan, Arya and Arya were happy and blessed to have a loving and caring mother. Being an elder brother Ayaan also promised that he is going to make their family so famous that the future generations would unravel the tapestry of lineage. All of the three siblings promised their parents to follow the rules of the family that were passed from their ancestors and even to carry on the family name. Their family was born with a silver spoon in their mouth because they were so courteous and gracious. Since then, for them blood was truly thicker than water.

# Beyond Tradition and Culture: My Experiences With SIMOC 2024

"Last call for Vistara Flight Number, V-115 from Delhi to Singapore."

As the announcement echoed throughout the airport, I felt a mix of excitement and nervousness. This wasn't just a regular trip, it was my journey to Singapore for a major Maths competition- SIMOC. It was a milestone I'd been working towards for months. The six-hour flight was a mix of sleep, gaming, and anxiety. I didn't know what to expect. As we approached Singapore, my nerves were out of control. My body was shaking with fear, while the scorching heat made me feel like I was about to erupt into lava. Exactly a day later, the competition started and I couldn't wait to face it.

I hit the jackpot and I was ecstatic to win the silver medal. However, the impact was far beyond the Silver Medal. I think the purpose of participating in this competition was not just academic pursuits but to broaden my horizons through exposure at such a big international platform. It helped me build on my strengths and overcome my hesitation. Sometimes, I felt tongue tied in first time social interactions but while working in teams with students from other countries I automatically overcame my fear. It was difficult to understand but fascinating to see people communicate in their own language. I got to know about diverse cultures and traditions. For the awards ceremony, we were asked to wear the traditional costumes of our countries. I wore a suit and holding the Tricolour while receiving my medal filled me with pride. The colourful costumes, interesting musical instruments of the Mexican students enthralled me. We were carrying souvenirs and delicacies from our country to be exchanged with students from other countries.

I also explored Singapore as a tourist and saw that there was a 'Little India' and a 'China Town' in Singapore. Singapore attracts not only tourists but also people to come and settle down due to various reasons such as strict law and order, great infrastructure, clean and green environment and good quality of life. People prefer to use public transport because it is so efficient and affordable. Since Singapore's National Day was also just around the corner, I also got to see rehearsals of their national day parade. The whole city was decked up beautifully. Their mascot – the Merlion was very fascinating.

As I reflect on my visit, I am reminded of how intimidated I used to be of social interactions but I saw how patient, courteous and receptive people were to each other's differences. I learnt to be independent and stay on my own with almost 2000 students from different nations. Each challenge I faced over there was like an opportunity I had, to learn new things.

Today, I am more confident and open to challenges and problems. I can stand before the mirror and confidently say, "I have changed for the better!"

# <u>Walking Into A Serendipity</u>

As I got off the plane, my eyes were met with a sudden slam of grey color. It was drizzling and the frosty rain penetrated through my skin making me shiver. I collected my luggage and left the airport. As I went out I saw black taxis and people were booking taxis from their phones. I was looking for Clea and her family in the big crowd. I saw the twinkle of a bright yellow- golden bracelet. Instantly after that, I saw Clea and her family. Clea came running and hugged me and told me that she was waiting for me. Her parents welcomed me by making *roohafza* which is a rose water dish in India. They were poured into flasks and handed to me with a smiling namaste.

As I looked around, I was surprised to see that there was no honking and the traffic was slowly moving. I saw that when people wanted to cross the road they pressed a button and used that to cross the road. In everyone's hand was a disposable cup of coffee. I was fascinated by the colors of the cups. This was such an unusual sight. I was used to seeing Indians with small cups of tea in their hands, as they sat and gossiped about the happening of the day. There were no street food vendors on the streets. There were only some lemonade stalls over there.

As we went towards her house we saw the house covered with green leaves. The house was eco-friendly. Outside the house's main gate, there were green leaves bordered with flowers. The house was full of bright colors. There was a foot mat in the shape of a tiger. When I entered the house I saw a large room. It was not a room but the kitchen. Everyone in the house was busy with their own work. There was only work in the kitchen in the morning, lunch and dinner. Looking at our excited faces, Clea's dad suggested that we should go for sight- seeing. We decided to take the red tour bus and go to Big Ben. This was truly the most memorable part of the trip.

Clea and her family asked me to wait on the bench near Big Ben. They had gone to get food and coffee for all of us. Big Ben is a clock known for its accuracy and massive hour bell. As we circled the tower and took in its brilliant beauty, we saw a young girl trip over a stone and fall. Her knee scraped the ground and started bleeding. As she had lost her balance, his foot slipped and got pressed under a stone. She could not move. Since I was in a foreign land, I was reluctant to offer help instantly. This is why I looked around to see if this girl had any family members around her. After I realized that she was probably alone, I extended a hand of assistance.

As I helped the girl to her feet and dusted her legs, I also gave her a drink of water. I incidentally had a Band-Aid and antiseptic cream in my travel bag. I used these items to tend to her wound. I asked the girl her name, and she introduced herself as Jenny Armstrong.

"I was supposed to be meeting my cousin and her new friend at Big Ben today. However, I lost my way and fell down. Thank you for helping me." She explained.

"That sounds wonderful! Big Ben is a great place to meet new people and hang out. In India, friends often visit monuments and famous places together. This is an interesting similarity between our countries." I added.

"Yes!" she agreed, as I proceeded to ask her the name of her cousin.

"My cousin's name is Clea and she was going to make me meet her new friend, Samaira. I think she is Indian like you." Jenny responded. I was taken aback to hear my name! Jenny was Clea's cousin! Less than a second later, Clea was by my side. She was immensely grateful for my assistance, and happy that her cousin was safe and sound. The family also expressed their gratitude to me. Inadvertently, I had lived up to the spirit of Indianness which involved helping others irrespective of who they are. Additionally, I had made a new friend and made a place for myself in the hearts of Clea's family!

www.ingramcontent.com/pod-product-compliance
Lightning Source LLC
Chambersburg PA
CBHW020652160726
47991CB00003B/1141